MW01600220

VOICES 4

An Anthology
March 2017

Website: bubbiepublishing.com
Email: faye@bubbiepublishing.com
Phone: 248-568-5797

ISBN-13: 978-1543230406
ISBN-10: 1543230407

Copyright March 2017
Bubbie Publishing
All Rights Reserved

VOICES 4

LIST OF AUTHORS

MURIEL ARNOLD
HOWARD GLEICHENHAUS
FRANK HARARY
EVELYN HOROWITZ
EDWARD R. LEVENSON
JEANNE LEVINE
GRCE MACCHIARULI
MORT MAZOR
FAYE MENCZER ASCHER
JANET MEIR
LARRY SANDERSON
DOREEN STAHL

TABLE OF CONTENT

INTRODUCTION

VOICES 4 is a compilation of stories, memoirs, writings and poetry from people who come from diverse communities in Michigan and Florida. The thing they all have in common is their passion for expressing themselves in writing.

The book's single purpose is to give everyone who has a manuscript to share, an opportunity to see their creation in a print book. Contributors paid nothing to be included and received double that in compensation.

Bubbie Publishing hopes to give all who write this same opportunity. It is my intention that the VOICES SERIES continue to expand and grow.

IN THE WORKS

VOICES 5: SPANISH RIVER HIGH SCHOOL

COLLECTING WRITINGS NOW FOR:

VOICES 6: POETRY

VOICES 7: POLITICAL VOICES

VOICES 8: GENERIC

VOICES 9: STORIES for CHILDREN

PLEASE SPREAD THE WORD!

Faye Menczer Ascher

DEDICATION

This book is for all
who love to write
and wish they
could be published.

MURIEL ARNOLD

THE PILL

THE SORROWS OF GROWING UP

WHO SHOULD BE THE FIFTH
IMAGE ON MOUNT RUSHMORE

BIOGRAPHY

The Pill
Muriel Arnold

I volunteered to participate in a medical research for a pill that, when swallowed, would make one 10 years younger. While I was alone in the laboratory, I saw the pills arranged on the counter, ready to be distributed to each contender. I took one, put it into my own pill box. Then said to myself, *If I took 2, that would make me 20 years younger.* I took a second one, but a voice inside my head said, *If you take 2, you might as well take 3.* I took a third one and put it in my pocket.

Fearful of being caught, I left the premises. That night I took all three pills with a glass of water. When I awakened the next morning, I looked in the mirror.

"Who is that?" I said. "I can't believe it." Not a line on my face. I didn't have one ache in my body. I felt like running out to the tennis court and look at all the old ladies I could play with.

I dressed myself, called my two daughters and said, "I would like to meet you for lunch."

"Let's meet at 3Gs at 12 o'clock," they said.

We did just that. They were already seated when I arrived. As I sat down, they said, "You can't sit here; we are waiting for our Mom. But you look just like she looked 30 years ago."

"Children," I said, "I am your mother. I don't know if the pills I stole from the laboratory will continue to work, but as long as it does, I want to enjoy it."

They looked at me in astonishment. Then said, "You are younger than we are. What if you don't return to you real age? What are you going to do? Take care of us when we get old? Are we supposed to call you 'Mother' when we look older than you? Your grandchildren will not know who you are; your great grandchildren will not know who you are. This whole thing is not acceptable to us."

"Janet, Sharon, I could sneak into the laboratory and steal pills for you also."

"Then what. Do you want to start yelling and screaming again because we come home late at night? Go through the teen years? What will OUR children say? By your stupidity, you messed up our entire family."

My bubble was burst. I sat there dumbfounded. *What have I done?* I said to myself. I left 3Gs. My children were angry. I would probably be banned from seeing my grands and my greats. Then I thought, *Eventually, I would have to go through the entire aging process all over again.* I wondered if there was a solution to this problem. I went home, beautiful, young – but miserable.

That night, I went to sleep; had no problem falling asleep; no aches and pains; slept like a log – no tossing and turning. When I awakened the next morning, and looked in the mirror, I had become the same old senior I was. The pills had only worked temporarily. How lucky I was to have exchanged my youth for the many blessings my old age has brought me.

The Sorrows of Growing Up
Muriel Arnold

She was a little girl who loved her Daddy more than anything, or anyone and the love was given back in ways that left valuable memories throughout her lifetime into her senior years.

Like the Sunday in the Bronx, the summer when she was a little girl. The neighbors gathered in front of the apartment building, wives sitting and gabbing on folding chairs, men standing around and chatting men stuff, and the children playing rope, games - whatever their fancy.

Muriel was wearing the dress that her mother had washed, starched and ironed. No jeans in those days; girls wore dresses with socks and sandals. Muriel wandered off to the vacant lot on the side of the building, curiosity, boredom, adventure motivating her four-year-old mind. Suddenly, a dog started coming towards her; she was frightened, moved backwards and backwards until she fell into a giant hole and emerged dripping with black mud all over her white sandals and her carefully starched dress.

When she walked towards her mother, she was greeted with a horrified stare, perhaps with thoughts of the washing, ironing, the extra work. Her Daddy took her by the hand, took her into their apartment, took off her muddy clothes and stood by the bathroom sink - rinsing, while little Muriel sat on the toilet seat sniveling quietly, feeling sorry for herself.

She then tearfully asked, "Daddy, do you still love me?"

He turned to her and said. "Of course, I love you. I love you when you are clean. I love you when you are dirty. I love you all the time." That was part of the precious memories that made the later sorrow more intense.

It was a sunny day…. Muriel was five. She was holding her mother's hand as her father boarded a train. She saw him looking at her from inside the train window. The train pulled out of the station and Muriel started to sob uncontrollably.

Her mother said, "Why are you crying - Daddy will be back soon." To which Muriel replied, "He is never coming back."

Growing up started at that very moment. Christmas vacation visits to the Veterans Hospital in Tupper Lakes, NY. Summer vacations when her father looked out from his window to throw kisses at her, dropping the comic-strip papers on Sunday mornings. The few times when he was well enough to come out of the hospital and take a walk with her, just holding his hand, that was all it took to make her happy.

Happiness and grief intertwine in one's lifetime, but intense anguish should have no place in an innocent little girl's life. It just isn't fair.

The most desolate part of growing up started when Mindy was nine, watching her Daddy in a box, being lowered into the ground, the sound of dirt slowly dropping on his head. She can still hear the piercing sound of her mother's voice, calling out his name.   No more letters; no more special visits with Daddy's little girl...Muriel's Daddy was gone.

Who Should be the Fifth
Image on Mount Rushmore?
Muriel Arnold

George Washington and Abraham Lincoln were chosen for their popularity. Thomas Jefferson and Theodore Roosevelt were chosen for their contributions to American democracy and the expansion of the United States. Their visions represent the Shrine of Democracy.

I pondered and thought, racked my brain to come up with the icon that would be best for the fifth image. I thought of Franklin Roosevelt, certainly a great choice; I thought of Harry Truman, another noble choice; I thought of John F. Kennedy... who, in my mind, would be the most mesmerizing face on that mountain. But would any of them draw the crowds that would revere the next face that would be a symbol of the heart of this country? Then it came to me. Why does it have to be a President? It could be anyone who was idolized by the many that represented the entire population of the United States, brought happiness and joy, without measure, into the lives of our people, a one of a kind. Of course!! It would have to be Frank Sinatra.

He was truly the idol of an entire era. His face on Mount Rushmore would bring bobbysockers back to life; the screaming, the delight, the ecstasy   There could be a sound system resonating from the mountains with "Strangers in the Night, My Way, New York-New York, All or Nothing at All". An endless delight, transporting people from all over the world to see a vision that represents, not only the gift that was given to the people of our country, but to hear the sound of his voice.

Would anyone scream with enchantment at Harry Truman? Not a chance! Would anyone worship Franklin Roosevelt? Not particu-larly. Would anyone swoon at Obama? I doubt it.

There would be no controversial recollections, Democrats and Republicans alike would be delighted at the choice - and the bobbysockers' screams would bring life into this patriotic site that would be revered all over the world. Most of the teen-agers today - and in fact, many of the adults today, when asked the names of the presidents on Mount Rushmore, would not even know anything about Mount Rushmore, nor would they know the names of the faces on that mountain - sad, but true. But everyone of all ages knows the name of Frank Sinatra.

I think it would be feasible to have a box office so that earphones could be rented to those who wanted to hear the voice of Frank Sinatra echoing throughout the area of Mount Rushmore. We would charge for those people who may possibly, not only desire the privilege of gazing upon the swooner, but being part of the vast audience listening to him. No lines to wait for doors to open, just sheer nostalgia, happiness and beautiful memories.

Additionally, I think the moneys collected from this venture would most certainly solve the deficit problem for this country and bring back prosperity to all. I truly believe, both Republicans and Democrats would see the genius of this endeavor, without question, and there would finally be harmony and agreement between the parties at long last. If this comes to fruition, perhaps Muriel Arnold, because of her contribution to the United States of America, could possibly one day be the <u>sixth face</u> on Mount Rushmore.

Biography

Muriel Arnold was born and bred in The Bronx as an only child. Her great love, her Daddy, went to a Veterans Hospital in Tupper Lake, NY when she was five years old. At the train station, she stood with her Mother, watched her Daddy pull out of sight and started crying, saying "He is never coming home." Her Mother was furious and said, "Of course. He is coming home. He is just going away until he gets better."

The years passed and the writing had begun. The letters were received on somewhat of a daily basis, always starting with, "My Darling Muriel" and ending with a drawing of a mother, daddy and a little girl with loving words surrounding them. Perhaps the receipt of those letters, which she still has in her possession, was the start of a future Creative Writing ability. Her father died at age 44. She claims her Mother was her rock, supported her with her seamstress skills, and made her the person she has become.

When she was 20, she married and became the mother of two lovely daughters, Janet and Sharon. They married and she is now blessed with 2 precious granddaughters, Heather and Nicole, their spouses and 3 treasured great-grandsons, James, Chase and Owen. Having been an only child, the growth of her family is a priceless gift. Her mother passed at age 56.

She divorced her first husband while her daughters were still young, raised them, taught them as best as she was capable of, worked to support them and claims, "I must have done something right. I could not ask for more devoted children".

After her divorce, she became an Administrative Secretary to an attorney. At one point during her employment, she lamented about financial problems that had always plagued her and prevented her from going to college. Her employer said to her, "Muriel, some people go to college and when they graduate, they forget how to think. You have a thinking mind that will guide you throughout your life." She never forgot those words.

She remarried in 1978 to Jerry, whom she adored and was not only a writer, but a poet and a composer of beautiful music. She had become an office manager for a multi-million dollar import-export firm. In her interview, her future employer said, "I need a right arm. Can you be my right arm?"

"Of course," she said, not knowing if she could. Through the 14 years, working in that capacity, she proved her ability, not only to herself, but to the boss. That determination and confidence has guided her until this very day.

Her writing in the past was strictly business, letters, no fiction, nothing that could be considered for publication.

Her Creative Writing class extracted her ability to write fiction. It came as a complete surprise, later in her life. The enjoyment of putting the written words together, to make an interesting story emerged. It is a wonder, a satisfaction and a delight.

HOWARD GLEICHENHAUS

THOMAS JEFFERSON and the BUNGALOW BAR MAN

BIOGRAPHY

Thomas Jefferson and the Bungalow Bar Man
Howard Gleichnhaus

Pop just appeared one day. We didn't know his real name so we just called him Pop. Nothing metaphysical about it, one day he wasn't there and then he was. Hard to tell how old Pop was because when you're ten everyone looks kind of old. He was definitely older than our dads and at least as old as our grandpas. So, calling him Pop felt right.

Pop's tiny ice cream wagon was parked along the fence directly in front of our apartment building every day from early June to the end of September. Pop, in a white jacket and captain's hat, pushed his frozen empire from where, we never knew. Ten year olds pay little attention to details, concentrating instead on important stuff like securing the fifteen cents for a *Creamsicle.*

Cooled by dry ice and loaded with frozen delights, the bright lettering along its side

declared *Bungalow Bar Ice Cream.* It was, in reality, just a push cart with jingling bells.
At first we only spoke to Pop when we wanted a cool frosty treat. Moms tossed coins, secured in tightly wrapped napkins from windows high above. White paper filled with nickels and dimes floated to and fro. Back and forth we'd follow its path, necks straining upward lest a strong breeze take it off course.

"What's good today Pop?" we'd ask. Each treat was pictured in all its tantalizing glory on a glossy card affixed to his wagon. Important decisions took time.

Our *Bungalow Bar* man, we eventually learned, was quite the ice cream philosopher. He could speak about the textures and nuances of dark and light chocolate. The subtleties of white coconut versus toasted and the value of double stick ice-pops compared to a single were debated in exquisite detail. Pop was the Aristotle of frozen desserts.

We also discovered he could impart other, much more valuable wisdom to our small coterie of urchins. He knew about parents and kids. He was clear on the value of school and teachers. Each bit of information was carefully imparted in a parable intricately woven around a kid named Giuseppe. Giuseppe did this and Giuseppe did that, always with some ensuing consequence. Pop spoke with an Italian accent, but the English impeccable.

By the end of that first summer Pop was more than just our ice cream man. In between stickball and street games or an occasional afternoon movie, we sat on the concrete sidewalk next to his three legged wooden stool. There were jokes with punch lines we never got. They were surely funny because Pop's ample belly would roll up and down with gales of laughter, the humor so contagious we grabbed our sides at the sight of it.

When our pal Gregory's dad was taken by ambulance to the hospital because his heart had somehow *attacked* him, it was Pop who put an arm around Gregory's shoulder and told him about the time Giuseppe's father had the same affliction. Somehow he got our buddy through those first critical days with a calm assurance that all would be ok. When Mr. Fried finally came home our Pop had Hershey bars and Dixie cups for all in celebration.

When Fall's first nip came to University Avenue Pop was gone. For a while we would listen from our windows high above the street hoping for the jingly bells. Fall turned to winter that seemed endless. Heavy coats and gloves, galoshes and corduroy pants became our daily uniform. School took all our time and summer freedom all but forgotten.

Then, on a warm Spring afternoon he was back. Sitting in my living room I heard it. At first, far away. Then, louder and louder the sound entered my open window. I looked down. There, six floors below, was the small white box with great big wheels. Pop was putting his three legged stool on the ground.

"Hey, Pop…up here…Hi…welcome back." I shouted. I wasn't alone.

Windows opened all around. The gang, Steve, Fred, Greg and Irv,Frankie, Anthony and Gilly were all waving and shouting. Pop, with a huge smile spanning ear to ear, looked up and waved back.

"Come on-a down youse a gang of mine." He shouted. "First a-one is on me. I got a special treats for ever-body."

Each of us got a hug and red-white-and-blue torpedo ice bar. It would turn our lips and mouths marvelous shades of patriotic colors. Our planet was back in its rightful orbit and all was well, at least until July.

Just after mid month Pop stopped coming around. We waited every day but he just stopped coming. No more stories. No more jokes or sage advice. All manner of speculation buzzed about.

Of course, the Good-Humor truck started coming around but we could never be disloyal to Pop. The driver tried to lure us away from our disposition to *Bungalow Bars,* but we could not be bought. Until, one afternoon a new truck made its way up the steep hill and stopped in front of my apartment building. It had a peaked roof making it look like a small house. It was a *Bungalow Bar* truck, complete with electronic bells.

"Hey guys", I shouted. "Pop musta got a truck."

Hearts stopped when the driver got out. It wasn't Pop. Some tall skinny guy with a huge, red bulbous nose dressed in white from head to toe stood there like a doofus. Even the goofy hat on his ugly head was white.

"What'll it be." he said in a sing-song voice. "I got it all, two dozen ice cream bars, eleven flavors of ices including lemonade. I got cups and sundaes. You ask I got."

We didn't want what he *got.* In unison we shouted, "Where's Pop?"

The new *Bungalow* man had no idea who we were talking about, but seeing that he was not about to make a sale that day, or any day in the near future, he ventured a guess. "You mean old man Prado…Gino?"

Gino Prado! Pop had a name. "Yeah Pop, that's him. Where'd he go to." I asked breathlessly. Expecting the worst, we held our breaths.

"He's over on Nelson and 180th now. Said this place was no good no more. Too dangerous if you know what I mean."

No we didn't. Dangerous? What was this fool talking about? In a few minutes the gang saddled up. We jumped on our bikes and peddled furiously to 180th and Nelson Avenue. Right there, in front of the Nelson Avenue playground was our Pop selling his frozen bits of heaven to strange kids.

"How come you came way over here Pop." I asked. "Some truck guy said we was dangerous. We ain't dangerous, no way."

"You got something wrong with your eye Pop?" Steve said, seeing Pop all misty.

"Sit down a my friends, I want to tell you a story about Giuseppe."

It seems Giuseppe had a paper route and he made some good money with that route. Tips included, Giuseppe earned seven dollars a week. It also seems there was bully in the neighborhood named Benny. On most weeks Benny would stop Giuseppe after he made his collections and steal Giuseppe's cash. Finally, Giuseppe gave up his paper route in the neighborhood and went someplace else where Benny couldn't find him.

"Hey Pop", I asked, "does Benny got another name? Maybe Patrick? Maybe Patrick O'Donnell? Huh Pop? Is that Benny's real name?"

Pop didn't answer. We knew though. Patrick, a neighborhood thug, sixteen, thought he was king of our street. There wasn't a kid who hadn't had his allowance money lifted by threat of violence from the crass punk. Parents were no help because no self-respecting kid would run to mommy with street troubles. You just took it and endured. This was another matter though. This home-grown thug was shaking down our Pop.

It didn't take long to hear the sordid details. O'Donnell and his sleazy gang were robbing Pop blind. Brazen, one would hold him while another lifted ice cream from the box. A word to anyone meant Pop's wagon might disappear. The old man took it for as long as he could then decided it wasn't worth his trouble. He moved on. We all felt terrible, and I suspected Pop was heartbroken. An old man pushed and bullied by a couple of street punks was humiliating.

Several days passed and Pops dilemma weighed on our minds. Taking on Patrick and his gang of hoods was not an option. We were eleven, no match for the surly, red-headed, freckle faced tormenter of old men and little kids. Moms and dads were still off limits and cops never got involved in neighborhood stuff like this. What Patrick needed was a dose of his own medicine.

Gilly's brother had just turned eighteen. When I mentioned it to Gilly he looked at me like I was insane. Sure, Myron Abramowitz went to City College, but dripping wet he must have weighed 120 pounds. Besides, a skinny Jewish kid from Bronx High School of Science does not fight a 170 pound Irish kid from the Bronx or anyplace else. That is unless he had a death wish.

"No Gilly,"I said. "I don't want Myron to fight Patrick. I want him buy us some wine. Then leave the rest to me. All you'se guys hafta do is get Pop back here when I tell ya."

By the following Wednesday the guys had scrounged together enough nickels, dimes and quarters for the finest bottle of Dago Red $1.25 could buy.

Bottle in hand, I made my way up three flight of stairs to apartment 3C. The little slot under the big brass knocker said T. Jefferson Sr.

Sweat poured out of me. I was about to knock on the door of the biggest, toughest scariest Black guy in our neighborhood, Thomas Jefferson Jr.

TJ, as we called him was not only big and black, he had a rep. Exactly what the reputation included depended on who you asked. Of course no one in my small circle would ever dare to ask. My dealings with TJ were always good. He would toss a football with me on occasion or run his long fingers through my hair when he passed. I really didn't believe the stories but taking a chance and going to his apartment was still a scary thought.

Laying out my plan to get Pop back sounded lame as the words spewed out of my mouth. I offered our gourmet wine as payment for TJ's help. The offering got a huge laugh.

"First of a all little buddy…"

Wow, he actually called me his buddy, I thought

"I don't drink wine. Next fall I'm gonna be DeWitt Clinton's numero uno half-back. Second, you seen that name on the door, Thomas Jefferson Sr? He's my old man. He ever catch me with some cheap-ass Dago-red the only place I be goin is to Morrisania Hospital. But, I'm glad you told me bout O'Donnell. Always liked that old ice cream guy. Been real good to me. Sometime's when

I'm short, no problemo. He puts me on the cuff. I'm in."

It took some doing and lots of pushing but we did get Pop and his *Bungalow Bar* wagon back to University Avenue. We told him it was safe and O'Donnell wouldn't be a bother anymore.
With some urging, an apprehensive Pop started jingling his jingle bells. We each bought a Dixie cup sundae then got scarce. Out of a corner of my eye I saw TJ. It was as ominous sight if ever there was one.

Thomas Jefferson Jr., bare to the waist, sat on a bench in front of our apartment building, Sweat beaded on his glistening black skin, dripping over rippled muscle after rippled muscle. Around his head, a red bandana tied with a knot in back made him look even fiercer. Dark sunglasses obscured his eyes. We waited.

O'Donnell came down the street. He was alone. TJ lifted his sunglasses and nodded in my direction. O'Donnell bit, he took the bait.

"Well old man, I guess you just don't learn.", O'Donnell muttered. "Think I'll just help myself to an ice cream and maybe few more for after supper. You won't be minding will ya, old man?"

Patrick pushed Pop aside and reached for the silver handle and opened the freezer compartment. He reached deep inside. His head was nearly inside the freezer box when he felt a huge hand clamp down on his neck.

"What the hell." He shouted. "Someone's ass is in deep now."

As hard as Patrick tried he couldn't get his now freezing head out. TJ pushed harder. Deeper Patrick's head went, until his face brushed against the dry-ice. He cried in pain, the sound muffled as the frozen carbon dioxide burned his pink skin.

Freeing himself the bully came up punching, until he saw TJ. Whether by instinct, fear or desperation, he took a swing. TJ caught his fist in mid-air. His huge hand grasped O'Donnell's and twisted until the mulling redhead dropped to his knees. In one swift jerk Thomas brought him back to his feet, driving his face to a nearby chain link fence. Then, with his powerful hand around Patrick's neck he lifted him off the ground, crying sounds emanating in choking gasps.

TJ's face, now inches from O'Donnell's nose, with feet dangling several inches off the pavement and his back pressed tightly into the fence he started to whimper aloud.

 "I'm gonna say this once you skinny son of a bitch, so you'd best listen good. You ain't gonna never, and I mean never, gonna bother Pops again. In fact you ain't gonna ever talk to him again. You ain't gonna never even walk on the same side of the street when he's there. You hearin me? Know what I'm sayin'?"

TJ let go. O'Donnell fell in a heap at his feet. We all broke out in spontaneous applause.

"And," TJ added for emphasis, "See these guys here? They're my friends. So if you thinkin' evil thoughts 'bout them, better start to thinkin' someplace else. Get your sorry ass outta here, NOW!"

We all hugged Pop who kept insisting it was just some dust caught in his eyes. TJ ran his long fingers through my hair and called me buddy, and made us all promise we would come to see him play at Dewitt Clinton.

Pop sold ice cream on our corner for eight more years. He continued to dispense Giuseppe's wisdom in liberal doses and we continued to gobble down his *Bungalow Bar* ice cream. He came to our high school graduation and was the guest of honor at the dinner our folks took us out for. TJ ran his heart out for DeWitt Clinton, went on to USC and a short but illustrious career in the NFL.

We kept in touch with Pop long after his frozen delight vending days were through. He went to live in a nice assisted living place just north of the city. One of us always made sure he had extra blankets and socks. Even though they got harder and harder to find over the years, there was always a supply of *Bungalow Bars* in the home's freezer.

Biography

Howard received a BA in Biology from Southern Connecticut State University in 1965. He Spent two years in research doing work on the biochemical nature of schizophrenia at the Nathan Kline Institute in Orangeburg NY and one year at Reichhold Chemicals in Sterling Forest NY as a polymer chemist. In 1971 he received an MA in Biology and in 1975 a second MA in Psychology. He spent 35 years in a teaching career in biology and biochemistry at the Clarkstown Central School District in New City, NY. Howard currently lives in Delray Beach, FL with his wife Fredda nee Kellman Married in 1972. They have two children, Corey and Rob and 3 Grandchildren, Alexa, Levi and Casey.

<u>FRANK HARARY</u>

MISSING PARTS

JOKE BOOKS

FORGER

DAN THE ANGRY MAN

HEIROGLY

AUTOMAT

BIOGRPAHY

Missing Parts
Frank Harary

I got up yesterday morning, went into the bathroom, washed my face, looked in the mirror and noticed my nose was missing.

I was sure I had it last night before I went to bed. It must have fallen on the floor. I bent over, looked on the floor and then on the wash basin, I even looked in the medicine cabinet. Rummaging through bottles of blood pressure, arthritis, and cholesterol pills, nail clippers, Emory boards and dental floss, but I still couldn't find my nose.

The kitchen, that's where it is! I had some Oreos and milk before I went to bed. Again, I started by looking on the floor. I found only dust balls and an olive pit in a corner, but no nose.

I pulled out the top kitchen drawer, scrambled between knives and spoons, found an unpaid electric bill and a peach pit, but no nose. Then I pulled out the second drawer, found a can opener, skate key, a kazoo, two double AA batteries, but no nose. Where is it?

Now I'm getting concerned. I have to find my nose. I can't walk around without a nose!

The bedroom is next. I drop to my hands and knees and find nothing on the floor except an old Playboy magazine and a pair of slippers. Again, no nose.

I look on top of the dresser, nothing. Then, I pull out the top drawer and find underwear and an "I like Ike" button, no nose.

I'm starting to sweat; maybe my nose is lost forever. Second drawer; socks, Jockey shorts and then, *eureka!* There's my nose...lying comfortably next to my...belly button!

I gently lifted them from the drawer, picked the lint out of my belly button, washed then dried them and placed them on the spots where they belong. That's better, now I can go to work with all my body parts intact.

I had a quick breakfast, looked out the window and saw it was snowing. The temperature had dropped overnight and I was freezing as I got into my car, then drove to the train station and got the 7:30 into Manhattan.

As I got into my office, my secretary said I lost weight.

I said "where?"

"Right there," as she points, "around your backside, your pants are so baggy there."

I touched my backside and felt nothing. I then ran into the men's room, pulled down my pants and …no ass! Now I'm missing my ass! I thought the good news is that it's a large body part and it would be easier to find.

At 6:45 p.m. when I got home, the snow had piled up on my driveway and formed an irregular shaped mound near the garage door. I got out of the car, then dusted the snow away from the mound, and there it was, my ass!

It must have fallen off this morning when I got into my car and said to myself, "it's so cold out here, I'm freezing my ass off!"

Joke Books
Frank Harary

I just got a new batch of comic books and can't wait to get started drawing. Let me get out my drawing paper and sharpen my pencils. My favorites are; <u>Crime U.S.A.</u>, <u>Detective Comics</u>, and <u>G-Men</u>. I'm wheezing and have shortness of breath due to my asthma. I've been out of school for three days now, and it's going to be hard for me to catch up with my homework when I get back. But, it's fun being home doing my drawings.

Ooh, I'm going to do this one first, gangsters in a car with one gangster standing on a running board shooting a machine gun; "Boom-Boom! Rat-a-Tat-Tat!"

Let me draw the flares and smoke coming out of the gun exactly. I'm going to use red and yellow for the flares, black for the gun. I'll use brown for the car and dark blue for the gangsters inside the car. There, that looks good.

I'm titling this <u>Machine Gun Kelly in Action</u>. This next one is harder to do. Should I draw it or not? I'm going to draw it. My father would like it. I'm going to use a whole sheet of paper for this. Wow, it took me a half hour to draw; very hard, but it looks good. I can't wait for my dad to come home and look at my drawings; he always leaves me a treat. What would I find under my pillow in the morning; candy, a chocolate bar, chewing gum, even money? Well, we'll see.

Here's my dad now.

"Frankie, these pictures are good!"

"Thank you Daddy." I'm filled with pride.

"I bought you a new box of colored pencils, now you can draw every color in the rainbow."

"Thanks Daddy, I love you so."

Maybe when I get better as an artist, he'll get me oil paints, brushes and a canvas. Then I could be like Michelangelo someday. Yeah, when I grow up, I want to be an artist. I don't want to be a gangster.

Forger
Frank Harary

Edwin spotted them the moment he stepped off the train. His employer, Colin Hayes and Colin's chauffer, Alfred, greeted Edwin as he arrived at Haverhill Station in London. Colin is the proprietor of an art studio that does restoration art and specialized artwork for wealthy collectors.

Edwin Everett Chapman is his top artist and has worked successfully on many previous assignments; Edwin's specialty is art forgery. He's done this for well over 30 years and in his small circle of artists Chapman is recognized as the top craftsperson in his field.

Edwin has forged dozens of Monet's, Matisse's, Cezanne's, and Van Gogh's and has fooled the experts. His copies have never been detected. In the car, Colin explains that a Russian oligarch—Ivan Petrovich, bought the "Portrait of Dr. Gachet" by Vincent Van Gogh for 110 million dollars, or 87 million pounds, two months ago, at an auction at Sotheby's Gallery. Ivan wishes to make an exact copy of the painting to hang in his home in Moscow and to retain the original for private viewings in his London townhouse.

Edwin and Colin agree on a price, and in order to get an exact copy the Russian oligarch wants to have "Dr. Gachet" delivered to the studio under armed guard so that Edwin can work directly from the original. The next morning as promised "Dr. Gachet" is delivered. Edwin is in awe- this is a masterpiece. He's never worked from an original before and may not again.

Edwin makes and "ages" his own brushes by using the hair from vintage fur coats, hats, stoles, or any hair born from an animal. He feels by keeping his tools the same relative age as the paintings gives them a special authenticity. He plucks individual hairs from the furs- glues them around a wooden dowel and attaches a ferrule that holds them together, then dips them into a thin glue solution for shaping. Some brushes will be pointed, square, wide, or thin. Edwin begins by laying out his palette, but before starting he adds chemicals to his paints to give them the patina of age. Using an 1880's raw canvas he begins.

A blaze of colors—red, yellow, green, blue, white.
His brushes spin with globs of color as he dabs tint over tints, bold stroke over bold stroke, and swirl into swirls.

Edwin works for many hours and as the northern light dims he is exhausted. A slight tremor in his painting hand, and diminishing vision makes Chapman's work tedious.

Edwin returns to the studio for many days over the next month and is now seeing his copy come to life. As he continues to paint— the Dr. Gachet portrait becomes eerily familiar. He notices a similarity between Van Gogh's brush strokes, his blending of color, his palette, knife work and his own.

As Edwin tries to understand this feeling he stops mid-stroke and says, "Wait, could it be?" Edwin takes the original portrait of Dr. Gachet off the easel, turns it upside down and carefully removes the portrait from its ornate gold outer frame. As Chapman inspects the canvas he is stunned and starts laughing hysterically.

On the right side of the canvas, the part that wraps around the inner frame, drawn in a pale, yellow, hue are the initials "EEC." Edwin Everett Chapman did this painting 20 years ago.

Now Ivan Petrivoch has not only one of Edwin Everett Chapman's portraits of Dr. Gachet, but two.

Edwin thought, *if only Van Gogh were here, Vincent and I would share a bottle of Absinthe and have a 110 million dollar laugh.*

Dan the Angry Man
Frank Harary

"It makes me angry when a dumb listener doesn't express real anger. This is dangerous Dan, the Angry Man—broadcasting from W. RAGE 69.9 FM on your dial."

"Ladies and gentleman, when you have anger in your heart, call me—let's talk about it."

"Let's take the first caller."

"Dan?"

"That's me – Dan the Angry Man – listener, what's your anger?"

"What gets me angry is my husband. He's a pig and he leaves clothing all over the house. He won't put anything away. He thinks I'm a slave cleaning up after him. I was so angry I choked him!"

"You did? Where is he now?"

"He's on the floor, unconscious — I think he's dead."

"Madam, you're my kind of woman – that's deep anger. Call 911 immediately and plead insanity – you're a sicko!"

"Next caller."

"Hello, is this China Garden?"

"This is not a garden – it's hell, you imbicile, what do you want?"

"A quart of wonton soup, an order of spare ribs and..."

"Hey, you're also an idiot. This is a radio show you putz!"

"Now a word from our sponsor. Attention – this is a special offer. Mama Gotges combination colon cleanser, energy drink, denture cleanser, toilet disinfectant and mouthwash has a money savings offer. Go to your store, grab a bottle of Mama Gotges and scream loudly –Dangerous Dan the Angry

<u>Man</u> and you'll get a 25% discount. Hurry, offer ends soon. Now back to the show."

"OK caller, you're on the air."

"Dan, I'm so angry – my husband came home at 2 AM. I told him he smelled from cheap perfume."

"You have lipstick smeared on your lips and hickeys on your neck Are you cheating on me?"

"No," he said, he was testing out a perfume that he wanted to buy me. Then a woman said he was hot and kissed him on his lips. The hickeys were an allergic reaction to the perfume.

"Dan, should I believe him?"

"Madam, if you do you should be put into a <u>straight jacket</u> – you're a <u>moron</u>, a <u>huge moron</u>!"

"Seriously folks, don't take your anger out on those you love – husbands, wives, family members, friends. Sit, talk and reason. Enjoy life. Anger leads to hurt and sometimes hurt cannot be fixed.

Now, if you believe any of that, you're a bunch of <u>moronic</u>, <u>idiotic</u>, <u>psychotic</u>, bottom feeding low life <u>imbeciles</u>!

Until tomorrow, this is Dan the Angry Man. Have a nice day."

Automat
Frank Harary

When I sat down for Thanksgiving dinner--
just weeks ago, I thought of the first time I
tasted pumpkin pie.

When I was 9 years old, my dad took me for
allergy injections to a place called the Essex
Street Dispensary located on the lower east
side of Manhattan. We took the Sea Beach
train and always rode in the first car so that I
could look out the front window as I
imagined myself driving the train. It rumbled
its way across Brooklyn, then over the
Manhattan Bridge and in minutes we were at
Essex Street and the dispensary.

After getting my shots (my arm hurt like hell)
we went to a Horn & Hardart Automat. It was
a fun place. A woman would dispense nickels
with extreme accuracy. You gave her a dollar
bill – you got back 20 nickels – never more,
never less.

Her hands were perpetually grey and I
wondered if they could ever be clean, or

might she die of metal poisoning. We grabbed our change and went to make our food selections. Looking through small glass windows, I saw a tall orange colored pie with a thick crust and asked my dad what it was.

He said, "Pumpkin Pie."

"I like the color-- I'll try it," I said.

We dropped in our nickels, turned the knobs and magically the windows flipped open. Then we took silverware and found a table. I grabbed my fork and was ready to dive in when my dad said,

"Wait – that fork and this spoon look dirty Frankie, get me two more forks and two more spoons.

I said, "OK Pop," although they looked clean to me.

I fished through all the forks and spoons and returned with new ones. My dad looked and said, " OK." I grabbed my new fork – sliced a piece of pie and plopped it in my mouth. It was soft and creamy with a spicy taste. I liked it immediately – boy was that good!

My dad finished his tuna salad sandwich and a cup of coffee and I finished my pumpkin pie and a glass of milk. Delicious! Then he grabbed some napkins and wiped our silverware clean, opened a small shopping bag and dropped the silverware in.

"Pop – what are you doing?"

 "I'm just borrowing" he said.

"But, isn't that stealing?"

"No, Frankie, borrowing is different than stealing."

I guess my dad was right, he knew what he was doing. After all, he was my dad. We left the automat, got on the train and went home.

The automats are gone, Dad is gone, but I retained the love of pumpkin pie and have inherited assorted pieces of silverware courtesy of Mr. Horn and Mr. Hardart.

Gentlemen, thank you for the memories.

Biography

Frank Harary was born in Brooklyn, NY and had a 40 year career as an art and graphic designer at various Manhattan advertising agencies. Upon retirement he started working in clay – producing many hand built ceramic pieces. His short story writing developed when he took a creative writing course six years ago. A proud grandfather of five, when not in Delray Beach, Frank resides on Staten Island.

<u>EVELYN HOROWITZ</u>

APOPEMPTIC

BIOGRAPHY

Apopemptic
Evelyn Horowitz

Okay, so recently I went to Washington D.C. Ostensibly, the reason was my friend; Laurie's son was being Bar Mitzvah. The real reason I went was because, Danielle Rothchild, called Danny by everyone, my nemesis from growing up was going to be there. I hadn't seen her in thirty years. Oh, I'd known what she'd done over the years, Laurie had never missed an opportunity to keep me updated: Danny built a catamaran and sailed it to Hawaii; Danny was getting her Master's at the University of Hawaii; Danny was teaching at the University; Danny had become a Buddhist; Danny got her Doctorate at Stanford; Danny was working for a Sun company in Palo Alto. I had never really cared about any of Danielle's accomplishments; I always wanted to know how she looked. "The same" Laurie always answered.

You know how when you're a kid you always say, "Someday, I'll get even; someday, I'll show them; someday, they'll be sorry;

someday, it'll be my turn?" Whenever I'd had those feelings, the person I most wanted to make grovel with envy was Danny Rothchild. In my mind she had become Fortunato, you know the story: "The beating Heart." "The thousand and one insults, I could bear no longer." Unfortunately, being civilized, I couldn't bury her alive. I'd had to swallow my envy and believe what was always my mantra, "She'll get hers."

Over the years, she didn't seem to be getting hers.

I suppose at this point a little background information should be supplied. It begins in suburbia in 1963. That's when I began to attend Chrysalis Elementary School. There were twenty four students in Miss Palmer's first grade class. We were the same twenty-four when we left Mr. Jackson's sixth grade class in 1969 to face the frightening world of Cummings Junior High. To this day I can give you the names of every one of my fellow students, but the ones you need to know are: Laurie Crongerg, Joyce Steven; my best friend until she died in an automobile accident, at age 24, Samuel Poster, and of course, Danielle Rothchild.

In those days, I don't know if it's true today, each of us was somehow defined by what our parents did. Laurie's father was a salesman, Joyce's father owned and operated a school bus company, Sam's father was a lawyer, Danielle's father was a dentist, and my father was a bookie. Mothers were all housewives who spent a lot of time driving children to school, lessons, friend's houses, and doctors. Often I would catch kids whispering about my father. I knew their fathers were always betting with him and often owed him money. They were just repeating what they'd heard their mothers tell their fathers. My father said losers always blamed their bookies. I knew what my father did wasn't legal, but Dad said it should be because government couldn't legislate morality, hadn't prohibition proven that, and besides everyone bets, or wanted to; everyone, except Danielle's father.

So off we went to Junior High: the smooth talker, the independent spirit, the judge, the studious scientist, and me, the outlaw. We, who had all been neighborhood playmates, now became preteens, The miseries began.

In October, there was a Sadie Hawkins Day dance, which means, a girl asks a boy; I asked Sam. At the end of the dance when we were sitting outside waiting for my mother to pick us up, Sam whispered: "Would you be my girlfriend and go steady?"

I, who had never had much use for boys, felt something warm and fudgy in my throat and chest, "Sure."

"You know," said Sam, "When you're going steady you have to kiss."

"I know."

"Good. Let's start."

"But my mother will be here any minute. She'll catch us."

"Um. Come over to my house tomorrow. We'll start then."

For a year kissing was enough, but then Sam wanted to do more. "We should touch each other." Sam said.

That soft and fudgy feeling for Sam disappeared. I didn't want him touching me, and I certainly didn't want to touch him. It became a bone of contention between us. Then one Saturday night Laurie was having a party, I had to stay home because I had mumps. It was about ten o'clock when Joyce called. "I don't think you have a boyfriend anymore," she said. "Sam left with Danielle."

Sure enough by the time I was well enough to return to school, the word was out: Sam dumped Elaine for Danielle.

Have I told you that Danielle and I were almost mirror images of each other? We were both tall, thin, I had straight light brown hair, she had curly dark blond, my green eyes bordered on hazel, and her blue eyes were almost gray. Oddly, local merchants called my mother Mrs. Rothchild, and hers Mrs. Gluntz.

"You know," I told Laurie, aware she would repeat it, "I wouldn't let Sam go any further than kissing. That's probably why he's with Danielle." I thought I was being very clever. I mean I never said Danielle's a slut.   It backfired on me though because no one could believe that Danny was easy, and that I, Marvin's daughter was a prude.

And that's how it went from then on.   If I went out with Norman Bass, a few weeks later he'd dump me for Danny, then Bill Dylan, then Murray Watts.   I got the reputation, and I bet Danielle Rothchild had the fun. At cheer leading finals it came down to me and Danny, the coach called us over, "You're both so good we can't decide. I've written down a number between one and ten who's ever closest is it. The other will be the alternate." You guessed it. She said three, a number I've hated ever since, I said nine, the number was two.

But the worst was when she was accepted at Wellsley and I was rejected. She said to me in front of everyone, "Oh it's too bad we

won't get to be sisters; I know how much you wanted to go to Wellsley. I really feel so bad for you." Everyone said wasn't that so sweet of her to say that. I didn't think so I thought, what a bitch.
Wellesley

I know all of this is very adolescent, but I think the real difference between men and women is that women remember emotional pain and men record triumph. Laurie and I always call each other on New Year's Day and ritualistically declare, "Chronologically I'm so many years but emotionally, I'm still a preteen."

Well anyway, to get back to the trip to Washington. Thankfully, my husband couldn't go as he was away on business, and who needs to deal with a man when you're about to confront the Cleopatra of your past. I flew down on Friday, staying at the Hyatt where the reception would be. I arranged for a cab to take me to the temple at nine the next morning, took a valium and a sleeping spill and conked out about eight p.m. Mercifully,

I had a dreamless sleep and woke when room service brought breakfast at seven.

Even on my wedding day, I didn't take as much care dressing and putting on make-up. I wore a navy Armani suit, a Paloma Picasso silk scarf fastened with two Tiffany bumble bee pins, Hermes shoes and bag. I was pleased with the results.

I gave the cab driver the printed directions to the temple. After studying the map for ten minutes, "Some idea I have," he said as he started to drive.

I have no idea why I always feel obligated to talk to drivers, but I do, so I asked my standard question, "Where are you from?"

"Yugoslavia."

"Is there still a Yugoslavia?"

"No, thank Allah."

Oh great I thought. I've got a Moslem zealot taking me to a Jewish temple.

There was no more conversation.

I took a deep breath as I entered the temple.
I saw Laurie's husband Dave talking to an
elderly woman and one or two other people I
didn't recognize. I headed to the ladies room.

Laurie was at the sink. "Ellie, Ellie you
came," she said as she gave me a hug. "You
look great. I'm so glad you came. Danny's
here. We'll talk later. I have to go, they're
about to start."

I took a seat in the back. "The better to see
you, my dear" kept running through my head.
My eyes couldn't find her. And then I started
watching a very thin, very bleached woman
who was talking to Laurie's mother. It was
the facial expression, the sympathetic little
girl look I recognized. She had grown old.

How do I describe how wonderful I felt. I
could have done one of those football end
zone dances. I got up and went over,
"Danny it's me Ellie. How are you?'

"Oh Ellie, how nice to see you. Here, sit next to me, that way you won't be able to sleep during the service."

Still a bitch, I thought, but didn't care. It was more like I was beamed up to the Starship Enterprise from the land of Medusa. It was like I felt the one time I was given Sodium Pentothal, I loved the whole world.

With a huge smile on my face I watched Laurie's son read the Torah. "He looks just like Laurie did at thirteen," I whispered to Danny.

Biography

Evelyn Horowitz is a former editor and publisher for THE BAD HENRY REVIEW. She began writing short stories and a memoir four years ago. She lives in Delray Beach and is an avid golfer.

EDWARD R. LEVENSON

<u>EDWARD R. LEVENSON</u>

PLACING JEWISH WOMEN INTO THE INTERSECTIONALITY OF RACE, CLASS AND GENDER: REVA SPIRO LUXENBERG

BIOGRAPHY

EDWARD R. LEVENSON

Placing Jewish Women into the Intersectionality of Race, Class, and Gender: Reva Spiro Luxenberg[1]
Edward R. Levenson

The main part of my title comes from an article by Jessica Greenebaum [2]. The need is to refute the prevalent stereotype that Jewish women are predominantly white, middle-class, and privileged[3]. Author Reva Spiro Luxenberg does this.

I consider one of her books *Grand Army Plaza*,[4] a drama, to be a veritable master-piece. It exemplifies the intersectionality of her female protagonists.

---

[1] Edward R. Levenson gave this talk at The Intersectionality Conference; Southeast Women's Studies Association(SEWSA), Winthrop University; Rock Hill, South Carolina; April 2, 2016

[2] Jessica Greenebaum, "Placing Jewish Women into the Intersectionality of Race, Class and Gender," *Race, Gender, and Class*, Volume 6, Number 4, 1999, pages 41-60

[3] Cf. Marla Brettschneider, "Theorizing Diversity from a Jewish Perspective, *Race, Gender, and Class*, Volume 6, Number 4, 1999, pages 12-23.

[4] XLibris, 2005

Grand Army Plaza, set in Brooklyn, is about an Orthodox Jewish widow, Chaya Bloom, who adopts an eleven-year-old African American orphan, Jamal Holden. Chaya had promised Jamal's dying mother that she would take care of her son. The theme for this narrative developed from a happening in the author's life when she was a social worker, a member of the Committee of the Handicapped team assigned to a New York City predominantly African American public intermediate school. One afternoon, at dismissal time, she noticed a diminutive white Jewish woman at the front door of the school.

"May I help you?" she asked.

The woman answered, "I'm here to pick up my son. He's small and I walk him to and from school every day because bullies pick on him."

Then Reva saw the son greeting his mother with a sweet smile. The work of fiction developed from that event.

The mother-son relationship in *Grand Army Plaza* struck me with great force, because it is a story of deep love and commitment, the highest universal values.

Grand Army Plaza in Brooklyn, after which Luxenberg's book is named, commemorates the Union veterans of the Civil War. Adjacent to the plaza is a side of the main branch of the Brooklyn Public Library, officially called "Central Library." Many Brooklynites refer to the library as Grand Army Plaza Library; and the author, in fact, named her book after the library, not the geographical area. Chaya Bloom's apartment house is not far away. She is a pious Orthodox Jewish woman steeped as well in Jewish culture, as reflected in her speech patterns carrying over from Yiddish and in her Jewish food preparation and recipes. Also, she is a Holocaust survivor.

The story begins in 1991, when Jamal Holden is eleven years old. He had been orphaned six years earlier by the murder of his father, which he had witnessed, and was to be orphaned again by the death of his mother. Before she died, his mother implored Chaya to take care of her son. Chaya's love and adoption of him followed.

The bond that developed between them was informed by deep respect. Jamal enjoyed the Jewishness of the household; and Chaya encouraged him to continue going to church on Sundays and to remain a faithful Christian. Hers was a constant fight against racial prejudice, which involved the animus of some of her Orthodox neighbors against her, as well as against Jamal.

Chaya had to deal with the criticisms of some African Americans that Jamal "should be with his own kind "In that regard, a professional African American couple wanted Jamal to come and live with them, feeling that they could provide more advantages for him. Jamal demurred because he loved Chaya; he also remarked that he considered them "Oreo cookies," black on the outside but white on the inside. If the author, through Jamal, has used a negative stereotype, I apologize for her. I do understand, however, that there is a "politics of authenticity" and that, as such, the connection between Jamal and Chaya represents a more genuine tie than that based on skin color alone, however important.

Whereas tension had been developing between Chaya and her daughter Fagele/newly Florence, who was distancing herself from Orthodox religious-cultural values, Jamal actually helped unify the family anew. Florence's husband Dave was principal of a Long Island intermediate school; and Jamal, who had been put in remedial classes in Brooklyn because he had been unable to concentrate, went to live with Florence and Dave temporarily when Chaya suffered a heart attack. Jamal made academic progress. Dave also suggested to Jamal that he should learn karate for self-defense. Subsequently, in fact, both Jamal *and* Chaya enrolled in karate classes.

Jamal had had haunting memories of his father's murder and went back to the scene of the crime where he caught a glimpse of the corrupt policeman perpetrator and his storekeeper frontman. They had been laundering drug money weekly for years. A plan developed—of Dave and detective friends—to wire Jamal and confront the officer. It required great bravery on Jamal's part, but it worked and the criminals were apprehended. (The policeman's name is Michael O'Hara; as a reviewer, I would prefer that the name be less stereotypically Irish.)

Besides the new togetherness of Jamal and Dave, Jamal met a widower rabbi, Rabbi Fisher, in the Grand Army Plaza library, and introduced him to Chaya, leading to marriage between them.

An important intersection in the book is that Jamal had written a book called *Dicky and The Dinosaur*. His friendship with Rabbi Fisher began in the library when the librarian recommended this book to Rabbi Fisher for a neighbor's sick daughter and pointed out Jamal as the author. The book was an imaginative child's fantasy transcending actual living cultures, embodying the ideal of multicultural readers bridging *all* cultures.

Towards the end of *Grand Army Plaza*, Jamal, a grown man now, who by then has received a Ph.D. in English, reveals to Rabbi

Fisher that he is writing a twenty-second-century story "about an Indian boy who finds a magic rock and is transported back to the time before the white settlers came." (4) I consider this story the symbol of a bridge to a pre-colonial Golden Age in the past before racism, slavery, and decimation of natives took hold in America.

There is a crime-story dimension in Grand Army Plaza's *dénouement* about the capture and confession of Detective O'Hara, revealing Luxenberg's skill in crafting mysteries. Indeed, three of her works are the Sadie Weinstein thrillers: *The Cereal Killer,* [5] *Murder at the Second Lily Pond,* [6] and *Curl Up and Die.* [7] (The latter is being revised as *The Beauty School Murder*.)

In conclusion, I hope I have succeeded in establishing that Reva Luxenberg is an important source in portraying the intersectionality of Jewish women. Her character Chaya Bloom illustrates

---

[5] Page 274

[6] Author House, 2011

[7] Writers Club Press, 2001

recognition that Jewish women have been very supportive to minority and Third-World people. Though light-skinned Jewish women "pass" as white women, many, furthermore,

identify as a Third-World minority them-selves. [8]

---

[8] Edward's wife, Reva, accompanied him and participated with him fully in the conference. It was a "peak experience" for both.

Biography

Edward R. Levenson taught Hebrew, Hebrew Scriptures, Jewish History, and Religion on the college level from 1972 to 1987. In 1982, he co-edited the first edition of *The Jewish Women's Studies Guide*. From 1987 to 2012, he was a high-school teacher of Latin and Social Studies. In retirement, he has been developing a writing career. He is the proud husband of Reva Luxenberg. His *"Edward's Humor" and More: Humor, Word Play, Personae, Memoirs, Interpretation* is forthcoming.

JEANNE LEVINE

CASH FIND

TARZAN - THE TALKING DOG

BIOGRAPHY

Cash Find
Jeanne Levine

When we closed our business and retired my husband and I visited Florida, checked out various areas, and decided to move to Kings Point. We put our house up for sale, and luckily, sold it quickly. Then began the task of sorting what we would take, what the children wanted, what to give away and what to just throw out.

We had watched our house being built from the first shovel of dirt for the foundation until it received the Certificate of Occupancy. We moved into that empty shell in October 1951. Now, 42 years later, we had to go through all the drawers, collections and memories this home held for us. Our children also had history within these walls. Roni had been 3 years old when we moved in, 3 months after Lewis was born, Mark came into being in June 1964. So you see, births, graduations, bar mitzvahs, anniversaries, family holidays were all affixed to our hearts and our home. Oh yes, in addition to the house there was a freestanding 2-car garage. This too was full of most anything but cars. It was mutually decided that I would start with the house and husband, Bernie, would begin in the garage. The children were grown and living throughout the country, at this time so we did not expect much help from them.

The decisions were hard but, in the end, we had 63 cartons trucking their way to a Florida storage where they would remain until we had our condo ready.

Back to our story.   Sorting, clean-ing, packing, perspiring (me who was always cold) was tiring for both of us. We were no longer youngsters. (Am I really admitting to that?) Shortly after one of our rest periods, I heard Bernie, excitedly, calling to me to come out to the garage. I ran, thinking he was hurt!

He was standing just inside the garage door holding what appeared to be a picnic basket. As I came closer I realized it looked like the old picnic basket we used when we went out on our boat.

"What's so special?" I asked. "We don't want to take all those picnic supplies to Florida."

Bernie couldn't speak. He just opened the lid of the basket and tilted it toward me. Inside, there was money, thousands of dollars of money. Most of it was in bills but there were also nickels, dimes and quarters. When we got over our first astonishment, we sat on the ground and counted the money. There was $40,000. in that basket.

"Where did you find it?" I asked.

He said, "I took the old dinghy off the shelf and, instead of our old picnic supplies, I found this money."

"Have you any idea where it came from? Were you putting aside money over the years?" I questioned.

"Come on," he replied "You know how little cash I handle. I come to you when I need extra money!" I knew, in my heart, this was the truth.

We thought and thought. Finally we decided to speak to the children. Mark, the youngest, denied any knowledge of the basket, but, he got off the phone rather quickly for him. Lewis, hummed and hawed, and wouldn't directly answer the question. Roni, our daughter, was on her way to visit us and help with last minute arrangements. As soon as she arrived we asked if she had an explanation for our find. We were just hoping it wouldn't be anything illegal.

This is Roni's story. The basket was one of the reasons she had come to the house, primarily to help us with the move but actually to make sure the basket was not ignored. She began, "When she and Lewis were young children Bernie and I tried to instill in them the need to save some of the money they earned. They made a pact between them that a portion of Roni's babysitting money or Lewis' money for mowing lawns or shoveling snow would be jointly put aside. When Mark was old enough he, too, was al-lowed to contribute. Even when they were working summer jobs they put some of the money hidden away. It didn't matter to them who gave more or less, they just were in it together.

As they grew older and were not always home together, they would send the one visiting the money they had saved and that one would find a permanent hiding place and put the money in it. The old picnic basket was no longer being used and it was chosen to hold their secret.

Their original thought, when they were young, was to share the money when they were grown. However, when we sold the house and were about to start a new life, they had a conference call and decided to give us the money for something to make us happy in our new home. They had no idea how much money they had accumulated over those many years until we told them. It was their gift of love and appreciation to us, the parents who had taught them what saving a little money can do in life.

Tarzan- the Talking Dog
Jeanne Levine

My children, from the time they were able to speak, al-ways begged to have a dog. Of course, the fact that Lassie, the TV show was in its prime made it all the more urgent that they should have one.

Neither my husband nor I had a dog as children and we did not feel the need of having an animal to take care of as well as 3 children. We tried to compromise and bought a huge fish tank, filled it properly with stones and a beautiful display of a variety of fish.

At first this was acceptable but soon after came the cry "A dog we can play with, teach him tricks, love him and he will love us back. We promise to help feed him, wash him and walk him." They used every argument in the book-relentlessly!

Finally, when they reached the ages of 6, 10, 13, we caved. Our friend had bought a dog for his daughter and she became allergic to it.

103

He offered it to us. It was a black Labrador Retriever and train-ed. Hearing the offer our children were upon us again and as I said, "We caved."

Those first few months they did everything they promised but Tarzan, the name he already answered to, and I became good friends. After all, I was the stay-at-home Mom and spent all those day time hours with him.

One day I was thinking aloud *What kind of surprise party could I make for our youngest daughter, Emily, who will be turning seven?*

To my amazement, Tarzan said, "You shouldn't make her a party until she keeps her promise to you."

Feeling like an idiot I asked, "What promise?"

"When you turn her lights out at night she immediately sucks her thumb. She has to get over that habit! She promised to stop sucking!"

Yeah! I must be crazy thinking that a dog can tell me such things, I sneaked into her room before I went to bed and sure enough Emily was sucking away, I never told her I knew she was still sucking, I only kept encourage-ing her to keep up the good work and stop sucking her thumb.

Another day we had another "discussion" if you can call talking to a dog that. Tarzan told me the friends of my son, Billy, my 10 year old, were up to no good when they were playing what they called "strip poker." Instead of taking off clothes they had to give up a cherished baseball card. Some of those cards had belonged to their fathers and were quite valuable.

I was absolutely dumb-founded! I thought they were playing board games or "Go Fish" something I considered normal. From that day forth Billy's friends were still welcomed into my home but they played their games on the living room floor or on the kitchen table. I just offered the fact that I enjoyed giving them milk and snacks as the reason for the change. They loved the idea,

What comes next? I thought. I'm sure Tarzan will tattle on 13 year old Joanie. I can't imagine what, if anything, she could do wrong,

As I was preparing dinner last night I asked, "Tarzan what news have you about my wonderful daughter, She has been so close mouthed lately." (Would you believe I was actually asking a dog about my child?)"

Tarzan yawned and stretched and said "Do you really want to know?"

"Is it that bad? Sure tell me!" I never could imagine my sweet, wonderful daughter getting into any trouble.

"W-e-l-l," he started "Joanie has a boyfriend. They meet outside of school each morning, hold hands. He is a year ahead of her in school and he asked if she would go to a movie with him. His mother will drive them."

I truly was amazed. I waited for Joanie to come home from school. When she did, she never said a word,

The next morning as she was eating breakfast she said, "Mom, I have something to tell you. This boy, Kenny, asked me to go to the movies Friday night. His mother will drive us and pick us up after the show. Can I go? Can I?"

Whoa! I thought, *My little girl is growing up!* Without consulting her father, I gave my consent.

After all, Tarzan would tell me if anything wrong happened.

Biography

I am 91 years of age (92 in March 2017). Since my life extends from the Depression to the present, I have seen many changes. I was born in Brooklyn, N.Y. and had a very happy childhood which included my parents, brother and my mother's mother and brother who lived with us. I graduated from Samuel J. Tilden High School in January,1942 as WWII broke out. I worked as a bookkeeper which helped a great deal when my husband and I went into the printing business. I met my husband, Bernie, at a block party, celebrating the end of the war. He had just been discharged from an Army hospital, having been severely wounded. We married in December, 1946 and had three children, Roni (deceased), Lewis and Mark. We have 3 grandsons. We had 55 years together before Bernie passed on. We retired to Florida in 1993. In 2007 I began writing a column "In Our Midst" for the *Kings Point News* which appeared monthly since then. I joined the Creative Writing class a couple of years later and enhanced my writing skills. I am currently launching a monthly interview column called "Center's Star" at the Weisman Delray Community Center. I thoroughly enjoy writing!

<u>GRACE MACCHIARULI</u>

THE BARONS

THE WIND

CHAUTAUQUA

BIOGRPAHY

The Barons
Grace Macchiaruli

I met a couple the other day
In life's path
Along the way.
As we sat pool side
Shaded and dry,
They shared their lives
Of times gone by.
Revealed some past
Which brought life's scar.

Who they are
So kind and loving
This couple be
They walked me gently
Home for tea.
We talked some more
And before you know it
I found out
Saul was quite
A poet.

He'd written volumes
Three short years
Shared the laughter

And the tears.
I marveled at Phyllis
Her lovely face
As he read his poem.
It spoke of Grace (not me).

So raptured was I
By their love sublime
I knew I would return
Another time.

When I returned, no voice had I
Saul read poem about Mother.
I began to cry.
You see she died
When he was nine.
Life without her
Was not so fine.
Then Phyllis shared
As Saul made tea
Of loss of son
Bright as can be.

We reached out hands
One to another
To comfort,
Calm,

Each to the other

I shared of marriage,
My daughters,
And son,
And of
My grandchildren
One by one
As we sipped our tea
The sun (son) shone bright
On an afternoon
That was pure delight.
They had
Once again
Touched my heart
That I hated to leave
But I had to depart.

As I hugged Phyllis
I heard her say,
"Give Saul a hug,
He's shy that way."
Again,
I knew
I would see them
Oh, so glad
To know 'em

I'd return
The next day
To bring them this poem.

Wind
Grace Macchiaruli

Light streaming through wind
Like a derrick lifts me and
Empties my course sand.

I love his whistling
Gently he purses his lips
And whistles 'Love Song'.

Chautauqua
I Don't Think I'm In Kansas Anymore
Grace Macchiaruli

What a curious place Chautauqua is. Everyone seems to be looking for voices. Can you see a voice? I never have, but maybe I will see one in this room called the Campbell Room. A group of tables in the middle of this long room divides it. And on them is a grand display of fruits, cereals and cakes and they all seem to be calling my name. With my tray full of goodies, I sit at a table next to a large fan that bellows, seat me, eat me, greet me, meet me, treat me, sweet me. Its cadence whirls like a whimsical song in my mind. Did all thepeople at my table and in the room enter the odd cadence? Do they hear the same voice I hear? Is this one of the voices they are looking for? Have we found it together, or am I imagining all of this?

At this point I head for the steps, thinking that maybe some fresh air might clear my mind. I walk down to the beautiful Lake Chautauqua. It's view like a luminous pearl worn on a queen's finger, raising her hand to be kissed. I am enchanted by her splendor, and sit at her feel transfixed. Suddenly, I hear different voices now. They are coming from the twin steam stacks of the Chautauqua Belle. Each stack is whispering in a loud whisper. One says "love" and the other "me." Over and over I hear, "love me, love me, love me!" I watch and listen in amazement until the grand Belle is out of view. Did the children and their parents at Children's Beach hear the voices, I heard? At this point, I wonder, *Does every inanimate thing talk in Chautauqua? What a curious place!*

I left the lake and met a tall lady in a green outfit. She told me to follow a long brick road. Unlike the Oz road of yellow, this one is red. So I follow the red brick road singing, "Follow the old red brick road," a tune I am familiar with since childhood. I stop to view some small children sitting on a stone fish in a fountain. The little boy seems to be riding it like a horse, while swinging a paddle. Then he lifts the paddle downward to use it as an oar and his fish becomes a boat. After he left a little girl mounts the fish. She sways from side to side like a water skier, then she raises her hands above her head and claps for herself. The next little girls hugs the fish while singing the song, "Are All the Bad Men Down in Colorado?" What a curious song! It's one I never heard before.

Then a mighty a gushing wind soars through Chautauqua as the sound of a harp playing yet sounding like a high pitched soprano voice. The duo holds me tight in a winged-like dance, elevating me higher and higher, until I feel drunk with new wine. Then suddenly the wind stops and a calm breeze barely audible whispers, "Walk with me, walk with me, walk with me." Then a faint sound of a piano key says, "Talk with me, talk with me, talk with me. Don't you see? I'm the key, rest in me, trust in me, I'm the key." Then the bells ring and the sun awoke from his short nap. He greets me with a sunny smile, winks and says, "Chautauqua sure is a curious place, isn't it?"

Biography

Grace Macchiaruli is a retired Para Professional. She lives in Delray Beach, Florida, with her husband, Michael. She has 12 grandchildren, six boys and six girls. Their ages range from 32 to 19. She has authored four books. Three are a series called, *THROUGH THE YEARS WITH GRACE*. The others are *THE YEARS GO ON, and THE TEA PARTY YEARS*. Her husband, Michael, did all the photography for these books. Her fourth book is a children's book, *IF MY TABLE COULD TALK*. Her youngest granddaughter, Samantha Tinto is the illustrator. This is Samantha's first published illustrated work. Grace has attended Mort Mazor's Writing Class at the Shirley & Barton Weisman Delray Community Center since November 2011. Before that she attended Mort's Writing Class at Kings Point, Delray Beach.

MORT MAZOR

THE TELL TELLS ALL

BIOGRAPHY

The Tell Tells All
Mort Mazor

It's easy to discern a lie from her; she has this "tell" "—a little unconscious movement-- where she touches her neck every time a lie passes her lips. I listened to this attractive woman who I judged to be about 55 years old as she alibied her whereabouts three nights earlier when she found her husband dead in his study.

His anthology of memoir and short stories titled "My New York 1939-1985…and What Happened Afterward," is available from amazon.com. His novel "The Drink Masters, is based on his 26 years working in the distilled spirits industry and is available as an

It's easy to discern a lie from her; she has this "tell" "—a little unconscious movement-- where she touches her neck every time a lie passes her lips. I listened to this attractive woman who I judged to be about 55 years old as she alibied her whereabouts three nights earlier when she found her husband dead in his study.

I'm Dan Davis, Detective Sergeant Delray Beach Police Department interrogating Mrs. Morgan for the past hour. I spotted the "tell" when I asked her simple questions such as "How old are you, Mrs. Morgan?"

When she said "35", she brushed her right hand on her smooth, sophisticated neck. I knew she had to be at least twenty years older. Every wrinkle in her lovely face and neck had been erased by the magic hands of Boca Raton's famous plastic surgeon Rafael Cabrera, noted for taking years off Palm Beach County's wealthy women through face and boob lifts. I've used him as a source of information on many cases over the years.

Morgan's husband was shot once in the stomach and once in the head. The M.E. took two 38 caliber slugs from the corpse. "Do you own a gun, Mrs. Morgan," I asked.

She hesitated a moment, then ran her hand up to her neck again. "No, I hate guns," she replied.

"So you came home around 11 p.m. last Wednesday night and found him. Is that correct? Where were you that evening?"

"I had a late dinner with a lady friend at 32 East Restaurant in Delray," she said, as her hand strayed to her neck.

At 4:30 the next day I stopped at 32 East on Atlantic Avenue when my pal, John Fitzpatrick, the bartender began his night shift. I showed him a picture of Mrs. Morgan.

"Do you remember seeing this woman here recently, John," I asked.

"Oh, that's Mrs. Morgan, one of my regular customers. She and her husband have drinks and dinner here often. No I haven't seen them for at least a month," he said.

"Thanks, John."

"Can I buy you a drink, Dan," he asked. "No thanks."

I drove to Mrs. Morgan's home, north on

A1A from Atlantic Ave. She answered the door wearing a long satin and lace trimmed black robe, a cloud of expensive perfume and a wan smile. "Detective Davis, come in. I've been expecting you."

I stepped into the luxurious home decorated with striking works of art, antique statuary and expensive furniture.

"Mrs. Morgan, we have all the evidence we need to prove you killed your husband. I'm here to take you to headquarters to sign the confession."

She motioned me to a seat opposite her. Tears rolled down her cheeks. Both hands remained clenched tightly in her lap, without a "tell" movement as she sobbed silently.

Biography

After 40 years of management positions marketing consumer products in New York City, Mort and his wife Lucille retired to Delray Beach Florida in 1987. Mort began teaching a course in "How to Write the Story of Your Life" in 2002 around his dining room table for the women of Brandeis University National Organization, Trails Chapter. He moved the class to Kings Point in Delray when he was recruited to teach in this community. In 2011 he switched to giving a Creative Writing course at the newly opened Shirley and Barton Weisman Delray Community Center.

Since 2008 he has worked as a free-lance reporter for the Sun-Sentinel and Forum Weekly publications writing about people, places and events in south Palm Beach County. At the end of 2016 415 of his articles were published.

His anthology of memoir and short stories titled "My New York 1939-1985…and What Happened Afterward," is available from amazon.com. His novel "The Drink Masters, is based on his 26 years working in the distilled spirits industry and is available as an E-Book.

Mort presently resides in Boca Raton, FL. with Lucille. In March, 2017 they will celebrate their 72nd wedding anniversary

FAYE MENCZER ASCHER

<u>FAYE MENCZER ASCHER</u>

THE PURPLE HEART

BIOGRAPHY

The Purple Heart
Faye Mathis Menczer Ascher

Mathew Yandura walked around a flea market in Jerusalem, on the grounds of the American Consulate, in 2014. He was only killing time and not expecting to see anything of interest. It was buried under some old documents when he saw it. He was not really shocked to see it, even so far from its origins. The most unusual things were often located in the most unexpected places. Picking it up, he immediately recognized the framed Purple Heart Certificate. [9]

"Where is the medal?" Matthew asked the stall keeper, who had no idea. The old man had never seen the actual medal, only the certificate. The medal was missing.

Matthew identified himself as a Lieutenant Colonel in the US Army, stationed at the U.S. Consulate in Jerusalem and a Professor of Military Science at Chicago's Loyola

---

[9] The Purple Heart award was established by General George Washington in August, 1782.

University. He asked the shopkeeper to give him the certificate so it could be returned to the family. The shopkeeper refused, "Business is business, even in Jerusalem," so Prof. Yandura took $100 from his pocket and purchased the award. He later said, "I would have paid $1,000."

The certificate said, "Robert Mathis was awarded the Purple Heart for injuries suffered for acts of bravery in Anzio, Italy where he ultimately died for his country on February 18, 1944." Robert Mathis was 32 years old.

Matthew knew well the Battle of Anzio and the story of the men of the U.S. 3rd Infantry Division who were the first to land there and opened up Italy and Europe to the Allies. It was an important engagement of the Italian Campaign of World War II. It took place on January 22, 1944, with the Allied amphibious landing known as Operation Shingle against the German forces in the area of Anzio and Nettuno. Many brave men died there, including Robert..

After returning to Laylola U., Lt. Colonel. Yandura spent one year, of his own time, with many false leads, trying to locate the Mathis family.

He finally assigned to one of the young ROTC Army Cadets, Jay Choi, a student at neighboring DePaul University, the task of searching for the family of Robert Mathis. There were a lot of Robert Mathis' to search through, but the original letter had been sent to Jacob Meyer Mathis on Duane Street in Detroit, MI. So he at least had a place to start.

For two years this cadet diligently searched. Then it happened, thanks to Twitter and his friend Gilbert Pacheo who upon his military retirement became a private detective specializing in missing persons..

In July 2016, this retired Special Forces Colonel and Inspector General Pacheco sent a Twitter message to Allyse Mathis Denmark, of Atlanta, GA looking for family of Harold Mathis, nephew of Robert Mathis. Harold Mathis was Allyse's father.

As Allyse says, "In this age of cyber attacks and scams, of course, my antenna went up and thought this was suspicious. But he explained that the US Army was in possession of a Purple Heart certificate for Robert Mathis. He wanted no money, and all he said checked out on Google."

Jay Choi got it right with Allyse. She is a great niece of Robert's. Mrs. Denmark excitedly wrote to Robert's still living family, including her mother, Ilene Mathis, her brother Evan Mathis, her several Mathis cousins, and her father's two sister, Gloria and Faye.

It was known by the family that Robert (born in 1912) came to the United States with his brother David, from Lithuania, in 1939 or 1940, leaving behind his elderly parents, Mordichai Matishevitz and Rashel Vershavska Matishevitz, his wife Eda and a young child. He had hoped to be able to bring them all to America as soon as he got settled. When the war broke out, his family became trapped in Lithuania.

The same year that Robert joined the US Army, Hitler sent his parents, his wife and child to the gas chambers. Robert never knew of the tragedy of his family.

Allyse spread the word of the finding of the Purple Heart certificate. But how did the certificate wind up in Israel? That was the mystery.

Because of the amazing story of finding the certificate and the correct Mathis family. The family spent months talking about the Family, about Robert, about other relatives, sharing bits and pieces until the puzzle was complete.

The trail of the Purple Heart was pieced together. Jacob Mathis, who lived in Detroit, Robert's oldest brother, was listed as next of kin to Robert. When Robert died, the Purple Heart was sent to Jacob. After Jacob and his wife Yonina died, the Purple Heart was given to David the surviving brother in New York. When terminally ill, David moved to Israel to be closer to Luba, his widowed sister and his youngest, and only surviving sibling.

When David died, Luba inherited the Heart. When she died, her surviving relatives must have cleaned out the Jerusalem condo and probably gave away or sold most of her things, including the Purple Heart Certificate. That is how it probably wound up in an antique map stall in the Old City.

Adding to the unusual truth of this story is the fact that although Mr. Yandura has been stationed in Afghanistan, Iraq, Israel and Chicago he is originally from Troy, MI. Like the Mathis family he has roots in Michigan.

The three military men responsible for uniting the Purple Heart with the Mathis family, Matthew Yandura, Gilbert Pacheco and Jay Choi arranged with Allyse Mathis Denmark and the US Army an impressive Reuniting Ceremony to present the Purple Heart to the surviving Mathis family so it could return home.

Since WWI, when the first Purple Heart Reuniting ceremony was held, there have only been 150 such ceremonies performed.

November 13, 2016, Veteran's Day week-
end, at the Holocaust Memorial Center in
Farmington Hills, MI, the Mathis family
gathered and paid tribute to their honored war
hero, and again received this precious medal
for their fallen soldier who barely spoke
English and gave his life for the country he
loved, America. The Reuniting Dept of the
US Army paid for a beautiful new framing of
the Purple Heart and the certificate.

Holding this unique and moving ceremony in
the Michigan Holocaust Center was most
fitting because so many of the Mathis family,
including Robert's parents, wife and child,
were victims of the Nazis.

Much like America itself, most of the people
who attended the ceremony from the general
public and from the military came from
immigrant roots.

Everything about this story is a tribute to our
amazing country and those who serve it.

The Robbery[10]
Faye Menczer Ascher

I was standing in line at the Publix on Sunday night when a man comes up behind me and points a gun at the cashier.

"Stop what you are doing. Give me all the cash in your register," he commands in the almost empty Publix, totally surprising the woman behind the counter.

Being third in line, the three of us senior ladies freeze at the checkout, unable to move or do anything, very afraid.

The cashier starts screaming hysterically, "Help! Help! I am being robbed. There's gunman. Someone help me." She looks at the three of us.

"Shut up, you stupid bitch. Quit that screaming." He started waving his gun around nervously. We could all see the sweat was

---

[10] This story is fiction.

pouring down his face making his ski mask moist and itchy.

"Give me the cash in your drawer, and hurry up." I'll shoot if you don't shut up," and he came closer to her threatening her with his pistol. Waving it wildly at her and us.

Not one of us moved. My mind was going a mile a minute. I was afraid to reach for my phone in my huge purse. I can never find it and when nervous have trouble using it. I sure was nervous now. I made eye contact with the other customers. We were silent.

Collapsing to the floor, the middle aged cashier, passed out.

Clumsily stepping over the woman who filled the area in front of the register, the gunman vainly attempted to open the locked money drawer. He did not know the passcode to open the drawer.

Frustrated, he started to run from the store, pulling off his irritating mask, his hair wet, his face red. The security guard was standing in the doorway, blocking his exit, his own weapon exposed and pointing at the robber. He was well balanced in a crouched position, both hands around the butt of the gun, pointing at the fleeing gunmen. His mouth fell open, he could not say a word.

"Dad. Don't shoot," the young man cried out to the security guard.

Farrell? Farrell? What in Hell are you doing? What's wrong with you? COMING TO ROB MY STORE? WHERE I WORK? ARE YOU NUTS? WHAT ARE YOU THINKING?

The three of us just stared at the father and son and this scene playing out in front of us.

"I told you dad I needed money to get my car fixed. I didn't know you were working at this store. I thought you were up in Boyton Beach. I need my car fixed. You wouldn't help me. I thought I could get the $900 from the cashier and get away and no one would get hurt and no one would know. It is the first time I ever did anything like this, Dad. LET

ME GO! I can just run away. What are you going to do? Dad, help me." Tears fill his eyes and he starts to sob.

Farrell drops his gun. It makes a deafening noise as it hits the tile floor.

"No, Farrell I can't let you go. You have done a terrible thing. Armed robbery. You are 22 years old and should know better. I can't let this go. I can't pretend it didn't happen. I can't pretend that you didn't do this. I am calling for back-up and putting you under arrest."

Sobbing hysterically Farrell slumps to the floor, grabs the pistol and shoots.

Biography

Faye Mathis Menczer Ascher, was born and raised in Detroit, Michigan. A school teacher and a social worker, she married her childhood sweetheart, Eddie Menczer and after his death, her current spouse, and love, Al Ascher. She has four children and two delightful grandchildren. She began writing for her two beauties, Emily and Finn, when they moved to England and left a hole in her heart, and 15 hours a week not babysitting.

Enjoying the publishing process, she started teaching others how to self-publish. The VOICES anthologies are her current hobby. She publishes these soft cover books, called VOICES as a service to the community. This volume VOICES 4 is the fourth of what she plans will be many more in the series, giving other novice writer the joy of seeing their creative scribings in a book.

BubbiePubishing.com is her website.

To Linda
My high school
friend, who makes me
look like $100. bucks
Love

JANET MEIR

BUBBE LAYLA

BIOGRAPHY

Janet L Meir

BUBBE LAYLA

The beginning

"No I don't want to talk to you," Layla Wassermann said nervously "Please, Go away"!

"I don't want to go away. You have much pain and sorrow, "said the Gypsy woman. Hanan "I see it in your eyes.   I could ease your pain. Please let me talk to you. "

"I have to get back to my husband. He's waiting for me," retorted Layla.

"Please come into my wagon, I will take you to him," offered Hanan.

Layla had just come out of the store. She had walked to the General Store to buy oil for the lamps.   It was a long walk from her wagon to the General Store. Layla liked long walks; it gave her time to think, especially in these cold Russian winter days.

 "I've been waiting for you to come out of the store," said the Gypsy woman.

"What do you want from me?" demanded Layla.

"Please," Hanan said, "I can feel your pain and the stress you have. I know that you're a good woman and I want to help you feel better. I can give you hope."

Layla froze. She thought Moshe and I could use a little hope in our lives. After our eighth child died, we have been feeling kind of hopeless. *A little hope will do lots of good,* thought Layla. *Maybe, it will be alright to go with this woman.*

"Who are you?" Asked Layla.

"I am Hanan. My people have a camp at the edge of the city."

"I am Layla." Layla knew Hanan was a Gypsy from the way she dressed. Before we go to your place; you must know, I have no money to pay you."

"I know this too, but it will be okay, don't worry. I don't want your money," replied

Hanan.

Layla became over whelmed with excitement. "I have to go to tell Moshe, right away."

"Okay I'll take you to him, come," said Hanan.

At first Hanan waited for Layla in her wagon, while Layla went to talk to Moshe.

"Moshe, I didn't want you to worry. I'm going with Hanan to her camp."

"Who is Hanan and why are you going with her? Moshe demanded.

Layla made a motion to Hanan, to come in her wagon. Layla made introductions

"Moshe, this is Hanan. Hanan, this is Moshe, my husband. Moshe, Hanan thinks that she can give us a gift of hope."

Moshe looked at his wife sternly and lowered his voice, "Tell her to go away; we have no money to give her."

"Moshe, she already knows this and she still wants to give us this gift."

"LAYLA!" shouted Moshe,

"Excuse me Hanan, I need to talk to my husband in private. Hanan went back to the wagon to wait for Layla.

Layla took a deep breath before she spoke. If she could make him see how important this is to her, he would understand.

"Moshe, it wouldn't hurt to have a little hope. She is a stranger and she is very nice and sincere. How often does this happen? Trust me, I will be O.K."

Moshe looked at his wife and knew that going with this Gypsy women meant a lot to her. His heart softened.

"Will she bring you back to me?"

"Yes," said Layla

"Here", Moshe gave Layla a loaf of Challah that she had made before they left.

"If Hanan can give us hope, I want her to know that we will appreciate it and are not beggars. Even if there is no hope, she has been very kind. Come back soon." Moshe walked his wife to Hanan's wagon   and kissed her.

"Moshe!" whispered Layla

"Go and be safe," said Moshe

Layla felt a bit embarrassed.

"I'm sorry; Moshe never shows his affection for me in front of other people."

"It's O.K. It is his way of telling me that you are very special and I need to take good care of you. Thank you for the Challah, it wasn't necessary."

"Yes it was." The Challah is a special bread. We bake it for our Sabbath"

"When we get to my camp, I will give you some tea. I make very good jam that will taste good on the bread."

Layla went to the Gypsy's camp, even though, she was still very nervous. The woman seems friendly and honest. But, how could she know about the pain, that we feel or the stress we have about seeing the Rabbi?

"I hope this chair is comfortable for you." Hanan offered Layla an extra shawl and blanket to keep her warm..

"Yes, I feel much warmer, Thank you!" Layla hesitated; but she had to know, and asked Hanan "Why are you doing this for me. You know I have no money to give you."

"Yes, I 'm aware of your financial situation. Your people and my people have a lot in common. Both of our people live at the outskirts of the city. Another thing we have in common is that each of our tribes has its own language, customs and own way of dressing. One more thing, you and your people are very respectful to us. The kindnesses which your people have shown us, makes me feel like we're kindred spirits."

"Like a distant family," Layla said.

"Yes, Exactly! I'm so please that you know how I feel. Do you feel the same?"

"Yes l do," said. Layla. .

After making Layla feel warm, Hanan served Layla tea, bread and her homemade jam. Hanan sat down to eat with Layla. Layla felt comfortable and started to relax.

Hanan said, "We should get started. Please let me see your right hand. I see there's much sickness and death around you. But don't despair there is also much love between you and your husband. You think the stars in the heavens do not approve of your union; therefore, you're on this journey to seek the advice of a wise man. "

Layla, push her hand away. She was amazed at the accuracy of this kind gypsy woman.

"Don't be afraid," said Hanan.

"I'm not afraid I'm just surprised and a little bit shocked that you know so much about me."

"It will be okay." May I see your left hand please?" said Hanan. Layla was excited to see what she was going to say next.

"You will have three healthy children, two girls, and one boy. The boy will be good with his hands." Layla was beaming with joy.

"Is there more?" Layla asked.

"Yes," continued Hanan. "When you think you can't have any more babies, you'll have another one. "

"Will it be healthy?" Asked Layla.

"It will be a healthy baby girl," answered Hanan.

"Oh, I'm going to have babies and they're

going to be healthy. Thank you, thanks so very much. You must take me back to my husband. I need to tell Moshe."

"But Layla, I'm not finished. This line" Hanan said, pointing to her hand. "This tells me, you and your children are going on a big journey."

"What about Moshe?" asked Layla.

"I'm sorry Layla, Moshe won't make it."

How can you be sure? Maybe there's a chance you could be wrong."

"Perhaps" said Hanan.

She felt that Layla wasn't strong enough to cope with this news right now. However, when the time came Layla would be.

"Where are we going?"

"Your family will be going to the New World."

You mean America?" asked Layla.

Hanan nodded her head.

"From your mouth to God's ears. I hope what you say comes true."

"It will, Layla, trust me."

"Thank you for everything. You have given me great hope. I must go home to tell Moshe. Will you please take me there?"

"Of course, I will," replied Hanan.

"Moshe! Moshe! I have some wonderful news."

"You're so excited," he said. "It's so nice to see you happy and excited for a change."

Layla told him almost everything that, Hanan told her.

"This is a good omen, Moshe. Isn't it? "

"Perhaps," Moshe said cautiously.

"I'm not so nervous about seeing the rabbi. I'm almost certain he's going to say that we should stay together."

"Layla don't get ahead of yourself. As much as I want to be with you, the rabbi has the last word. We agreed remembered."

"Yes Moshe, I remember, but now I have hope. You should too."

It was a big synagogue. A nice lady took us to the rabbi's office. Moshe told him about the death of our children and why we needed his advice.

"You have told me all the reasons why you think you shouldn't be together. Now tell me why you should be together," the rabbi said.

Moshe spoke first. "After the death of our eighth child, we cried and grieved together. We held each other because we didn't know what else to do. Only Layla knows what I've been through. She completes me. I don't want to go on without her."

"Layla, how do you feel? the Rabbi asked.

"Not once, did Moshe blame me for the death of our children.   Sometimes, a husband will blame his wife for things that have gone wrong in a marriage, especially the death of a child. I know. I have seen this happened. Moshe was wonderful. He saw and felt my pain. Moshe held and comforted me each time. I love him and he completes me."

"You two have a strong love for each other. It bonds you together in a very special way," the Rabbi said. "Would you sacrifice your love for each other? If I said that the death of your children was a bad omen and it is a message from God that you two should not be together. Would you get a geit?"[11]

"Yes!" Layla and Moshe said together.The room was quiet and full of tension. Finally, the Rabbi spoke.

"Your Faith in God is all He asks of you. Whether you stay together or not, must be

---

[11] A traditional Jewish divorce

your decision not God's." Layla and Moshe were delirious with joy.

"Thank you.   Thank you very much," they said together.

"Moshe! Moshe! I told you the rabbi was going to tell us that we should be together."

"He didn't quite say that. He said we should decide what we want to do."

"Yes! Yes! But we still love each other and this time it will be different."

"Why?" asked Moshe,

"Because of the Gypsy woman. She gave us hope. It's a gift. I'm not going to waste it. To make sure the children will stay alive I'll make a pact with God. I will fast two day every week until I die."

"Layla, you don't have to do this," Moshe protested.

"**Yes I do!** Moshe."

Layla reached for Moshe's hand. "Just promise me that you will love me and support the things that I do. I'm doing this for our family."

"Of course, I will. I just worry about your health".

"Don't worry about me. I'm a very strong woman."

"I know. It's one of the many things that I love about you."

Journey to America

Layla's' children sent for her and their youngest sister, Gussie, to come to America.

It's just like Hanan said it would be. All my children are in America. Now it is time for Gussie and me to go. It's too bad Moshe got sick and died last year. I so hopped, that Hanan would be wrong about Moshe, Layla thought.

"Mama, why are you just sitting and thinking? We have so much to do, our visas have finally come," said Gussie.

"Slow down, Gussie, we have plenty of time."

"**Time!** We have only two days to pack everything in this one trunk. I hope we can fit everything into this great big trunk," said Gussie.

"This trunk is for the both of us. I'm sure we'll manage," replied Layla.

"Didn't we use to have more suitcases?" asked Gussie.

"Not really, your brother, bless his heart, made suitcases for himself and your sisters. Whatever Benjamin makes is strong and beautiful. His hands are magic."

"I know mama, it's just like the old Gypsy woman said, that he would be very talented with his hands. Mama did the old Gypsy woman ever say anything about my talents?"

"No! Only that you were my last blessing."

"Thanks" mama.

Gussie Goes to Heaven

Silka, Rochelle, Benjamin, Mama and Papa everyone is here. We're one big family again, Gussie thought.

"Oh, Mama and Papa I'm so happy to see you again."

"**Gussie!**" Mama said sternly,

Oh, Oh! Now what did I do? Mama sounds very upset with me, Gussie thought.

"Didn't you see the truck coming? I could have waited to see you. "

"No! Mama, I didn't see the truck. I had other things on my mind."

"Oh Gussie, You never look to see what's going on. You just jump right into things."

"But, Mama I did well with the children you remember Rifcha and Morris?"

"Of course I do," replied Mama. "I used to baby sit for them."

Gussie couldn't wait to tell Mama about all of her children.

"Rifcha is so smart and pretty, Morris's is an electrician. He is good with his hands just like Uncle Benjamin. And of course, there is Lily the one we named after you. She's very pretty and she married well. All my children have children now. Rifcha's boy, Barry is the first to go to college. Mama, will the other children go to a university?"

Mama smiled at her youngest daughter and said, "I don't know, Gussie, we don't see the future here. We tried to give a helping hand every now and then. We'll have to wait and see". Mama continued, "Two marriages after Raffel?"

Mama didn't seem happy with the choices I made, thought Gussie. "Mama, I was lonely and I was very fond of both of them. You know the love of my life is Raffel. He wasn't my first, but love is sweeter the second time."

"Speaking of Raffel, he has been waiting to see you Gussie." Mama was pointing to someone. Gussie was so happy to see her husband, the father of her children.

"Oh Raffel, you're so handsome. Just the way I remember you. I missed you so much."

"My Goldie, (Gussie's American name) you're beautiful. Even up here, your beauty takes my breath away."

"Raffel you always had my heart." She felt his energy, warmth and essence move in her. For a moment, they became one entity.

Biography

I grew up in the Detroit area. I married an Israeli man. We produced two bright and successful children. They have given us four beautiful and smart granddaughters. I am a retired Special Education Teacher. I taught the mentally impaired children, in Detroit, for 22 years. Right now, I volunteer in a literacy program, in the Detroit area. I like to spend my time traveling and being with my family.

LARRY SANDERSON

GO WEST YOUNG MAN , GO WEST...OOOPPS!!!

BIOGRAPHY

GO WEST YOUNG MAN ,
GO WEST...OOOPPS!!!
Larry Sanderson

This is a story about an ADVENTURE of sorts. Not the typical adventure...no great conquest of the seas, nor riding in a wagon train over hills and dale, but just how a life has progressed for one aggressive adventurer.

Let's give you a little history.

My name is Larry Sanderson. I am a senior citizen in my seventh decade and am one of those dreaded Red Sox fans as I was born and brought up in that small but lovely city to the North. I am an accountant by education, experience etc. turned entrepreneur in 1977 and retired after having sold draperies, window treatments, bedding etc. to some of our finest hotels for the last 20 years of my working existence. Does this have anything to do with "GO WEST", ...no but what the hell, figured it adds color to the story.

In 2011, while living in the Naples area, ON THE WEST COAST OF FLORIDA, I separated from my wife and divorced in 2012.

Those of you who are divorced or widowed know that this leads you into the strange world of 'singledom'. It means starting a whole new life, not just seeking companionship, should you choose, but generally the need to set up house-keeping, purchase furniture, accessories, dishes, linens, etc. etc. I use the expression that it is a PITA. That's an acronym for a "pain in the ass". If you are smart and have the option to stay or be with your wife, 'significant other' (S.O.). or any other, it is a better option than trudging out on your own into this cruel world. In any event, those of us out in that single world generally do well. Men, as we all know, do not do well shopping, however they do get a certain amount of respect from sales clerks who fear their 'masculinity' which we all know as grouchiness.

Back to the story...I do get sidetracked sometimes. So, in 2012 having realized and accepted that I wanted to set out on a new life, I began exploring 'how to be single'. I first went to the known haunts such as restaurants, nightclubs to see what may be available in the so called 'meet market'. I soon realized that that was a waste of time so I looked into online dating. There I found a multitude of options, some very fat, some very thin, many who lied about their age, their background, published pictures that may have been as much as 20 years old, etc. etc. But I was determined to meet someone who could be what I called a "compatible companion". You have to realize and accept that after all these years you can't get EVERYTHING you would like. Therefore, the key word is compromise.

BTW[12], just a couple of tips for anybody that ends up single, 1) buy or borrow a dog and take it out for a walk, women are drawn to men with dogs, also 2) spend your time in a Super Market asking questions about food, etc. Good way to meet prospective dates.

---

[12] By The Way

Probably the first two years into my single life, I realized that the one area I could not compromise in was religion. I wanted to meet a nice Jewish woman, a woman who would understand *yuts* and *shmuck*, *shmegegy* and those thousands of terms, we of the Jewish faith, were all brought up with. If I said to an Irish woman, that guy's a *yuts*, she would look at me as if I had two heads. She didn't have to be great at sex, cooking, etc.(although being good at it was a bonus) but had to know the 'language'.

So, I spoke to, met, dated many women, some who I had some chemistry with and some not. I also met many women who I thought had potential, but they did not see me as a 'compatible companion'. I can't understand that because I, of course, think I am a great catch, yuk yuk.

So after about three years of arduously trying to find that elusive mate on the West coast, I made a life changing decision to "GO EAST YOUNG MAN, GO EAST" and moved to Delray Beach and rented in Glen Eagles Condo Community. I knew the area somewhat (as I had made a mistake of dating some women in that area while living in the Naples area) and was told it was a good area to find that sweetheart I was searching for.

I am happy to tell you that only a month and a half after moving to Delray, I knew I had found a companion that is so sweet, so beautiful, so smart, that I could not be happier. She lights up my life and do I thank the world for leading me to her. WE are both very happy and spending wonderful quality time together. It shows that with persistence and patience life can bring you the happiness we all deserve.

Biography

I was born in 1939 in a Jewish 'Ghetto" area known as Roxbury/Dorchester. Everybody I knew and dealt with were of the same faith. It was a great life as I knew it, never expecting much, never needing much other than three squares a day and a place to sleep. My parents were working class, however every summer we went away for the summer to a different vacation area in the northeast.

I graduated from high school in 1956, made a sad mistake and enlisted in the U.S. Navy for three and a half years. What a waste! After the Navy, I went to Bentley College in Boston and graduated with a Bachelor's Degree in accounting. I was in accounting for about 13 years and then was asked to join a company being formed in the Framingham, MA area as a principal. Eventually I went out on my own and from 1981 to 2010, I had my own company selling various products, the last being draperies and window treatments to many upscale hotels in the northeast.

From a personal standpoint, I was married twice, therefore divorced twice. I have two married biological kids and 4 grandchildren.

Health wise, I am very lucky in that I am very healthy, have no issues, have had a couple of elective surgeries. I exercise 3 times a week, eat reasonably healthy, am a believer in dietary supplements and am nonconfrontational (although my second wife might disagree).

Activity wise, I play golf, exercise and walk regularly. I attend and participate in many discussion groups, play cards and spend a lot of time with my Significant Other (S.O.) going to theaters, plays, traveling etc.

I believe in my religion, although I am not an active participant.

In 2013 I formally retired and am now a resident of Delray Beach, Florida.

<u>DOREEN STAHL</u>

MY MIRROR

THE MOON

THE RAIN DROP

BIOGRAPHY

My Mirror
Doreen Stahl

As children, we seldom looked into a mirror.
Growing up as teenagers
We hate to look at our complexion.
"It's normal" the folks say.
"We all had breakouts.
Who cares about them?"
When the makeup rituals start,
We never stop looking.
"You look fabulous," everyone would say.
Nude, I would see my body forming into a
Voluptuous state, in my eyes.
Conceit turns to fear as we age.
I still look good, I try to believe.
When they give you senior prices
Without checking, then it begins.
Buying every wrinkle cream invented, l try.
A waitress says, "You look beautiful, Mama.
Ahh, there's the rub.
My body is not fat.
But tell that to the extra skin
On my thighs and stomach.
Where did my backside go?
Now it's flatter and flatter, ugh.
Well it is what it is.

My mirror shows all.

The Moon
Doreen Stahl

As I gaze upon the heavens
What a wonderful luxurious sight.
As l see the moon drifting
Through the dark and dingy night.
When it fades, I feel the sadness
Of a long departed friend.
But when it brightens up the heavens
I feel so gay again.
As if I was the one sailing
Through oceans of cloudy mists.
Extending a golden light to fade away
And no more to exist.

The Rain Drop
Doreen Stahl

Drip drop, drip drop
Merrily about its work
Is a rain drop
Which is gaily refreshing the earth.
Making land so fertile,
Keeping dryness out.
A rain drop is a secret treasure
Man couldn't be without.

Biography

I was born in Philadelphia, Pennsylvania. My mother
Anna and my father Al Miller named me Doreen
Joan. My sister Marilyn is one and a half years older
than me, and all my life she has been my protector.
When I was very young my parents moved to
Brooklyn, to a three story apartment building. I went
all thru my schooling in my neighborhood. I took
ballet at Carnegie Hall. I also joined a modern dance
class in my school. I met the love of my life, Joe
Stahl, when I was 13 years old.

After I graduated from high school I went to work as
a legal secretary in Manhattan. While I was working,
I attended City College at night. My love for dancing
paid off because I won a dance contest and was
offered a job with a professional Latin troop. At the
Pines Hotel I taught dancing and performed in all of
the Latin shows. I also performed at the Concord and
Raleigh Hotels in the Catskills. The Band at the Pines
was Joe Cuba.

Joe Stahl and I married in 1960 and he will always
be the love of my life. We had a great marriage and
traveled through Europe and Asia.

My son Jody was born in 1963 and he made our life
complete. After Jody was born I decided to pursue
another career and went into sales. We lived in

Howard Beach and then my husband's job took us to Dallas. My son graduated from high school in Texas. My husband received a job offer from his prior boss and we moved to Indianapolis. Jody attended college at C.W. Post in New York. After a year in Indiana we relocated back to New York.

In 2007 Joe retired and we moved to Delray Beach, Florida where we still reside.

Through my entire life and many careers, I have always had a deep love for poetry.

OTHER BOOKS by BUBBIE PUBLISHING
Faye Menczer Ascher

KEEPING PROMISES TO MYSELF
My Self-Publishing Journal
Getting It Done Journal
10 Easy Steps to Self-Publishing

CHILDREN'S BOOKS
How the Zebra Gets Her Stripes
How the Snail Gets Its Shell
How the Elephant Gets Its Ears
How the Camel Gets Its Hump
110 Knock Knock Jokes: Letter A
A to Z Knock Knock Jokes
Playing All Day Long
We Love Trains

VOICES
VOICES	Michigan Writers
VOICES 2	U.S. Writers
VOICES 3	Florida Weisman Seniors
VOICES 4	MI and FL Writers
VOICES 5	Spanish River High School

OTHER TITLES
Bridge of Memories	Martin Cohen
Teaching is Murder	Diane Bernstein

<u>VOICES SERIES</u>

It is 100% free to be published in a VOICES anthology. There is no cost and no compensation. If you would like to be included contact Faye Menczer Ascher
Email: faye@bubbiepublishing.com
Call: 248-568-5797
Visit our website: bubbiepublishing.com

Collecting material now for
UP COMING VOICES

POET VOICES 6
POLITICAL VOICES 7
VOICES 8 – undecided

March 2017
All rights reserved

VOICES 4

Bubbie Publishing:
How it Came to Be

In Feb 2014, my two beautiful grandchildren moved to England and I was left with a hole in my heart and 15 hours a week when I was not baby-sitting. Wanting to use that time constructively and to keep close to the little ones, I decided to write picture books and illustrate them using internet artwork.

I was a novice at both writing and using the computer. That needed to change. The Apple Store became my new hangout center and writing groups my new companions.

The first book was completed as a Snapfish® photo album, was called *A Kangaroo Problem* and was printed in May 2015. Nine more books quickly followed. Being a proud new author, my friends wanted to support me and buy the books for their grandkids.

"They are not for sale," I said, "They are only for Emily and Finn."

"You should publish them for the public," I was told. So, I did and Bubbie Publishing was born. In March 2016 my first Amazon.com book for Kindle, *A-Z Knock Knock*

Jokes, became available thanks to a lot of work from my son and editor, Mike Menczer. A dozen more physical books followed for both adults and kids.

Collaborating with a terrific artist from Vietnam, Phanminhtuan, I was very careful that all the art work was original and not protected by copyright.

Publishing, more than writing became my new passion. There were so many folks writing delightful narratives who did not have the whatever to publish. I decided Bubbie Publishing would be their publisher. It would be another one of my volunteer projects. No one would pay to be included and I would do the work.

A book would be produced that anyone who wished to be included, could be, and anyone could be an author. The book would be available to the public through Amazon and CreateSpace. Their writings would be public for all to see. Plus, importantly, all authors could keep the rights to their own work.

The VOICES project was born. Of the eleven authors six I knew, and the others were strangers who heard about the anthology and emailed their manuscripts and I never met them.

It is the intention of Bubbie Publishing to keep producing these VOICES works as-long as there are people who wish to be included.

If you, or anyone you know, would like to be part of VOICES please contact me through bubbiepublishing.com or call me at 248-568-5797. Come join our VOICES family.

Faye Menczer Ascher

VOICES 4

VOICES 4

VOICES 4

67301664R00110

Made in the USA
Lexington, KY
07 September 2017